THIRTY POEMS
jehane markham

Published by Rough Winds

CONTENTS

DAYS OF THE WEEK	4
PARADELLE FOR KEATS	6
COLERIDGE AT GRETA HALL, 1802	7
SNOW AND PASTERNAK	8
FRANK SINATRA	10
FRANK SINATRA DECONSTRUCTED	11
IF YOU NEVER GROW UP	12
FEAR OF FALLING	13
LONDON BLUES	14
PARADISE BEACH	16
YANI'S PARLOUR	18
SONG TO HERMES	20
THE WEDDING	21
FEBRUARY IS A GREEN MONTH	22
SHE KEEPS THREE CATS	23
WATER AND STONES	24
THE RAINY SEASON	25
TUOL SLENG	26
CAMBODIAN SMILE	28
HOTEL ROYALE	29
NOW IN MY ENGLISH GARDEN	30
LEAVING YOU	31
MEMOIRS OF AN OPIUM PIPE	32
MR. CUNG	33
THE RAGS OF MY DREAMS	34
LAST SESSION	35
SISTERS	36
GHOSTS	37
SWANS	42
VALENTINE	43

DAYS OF THE WEEK

Monday, pearly grey,
Paris roof tops, I cling to the ridge tiles
with the pink claws of a dove.

Tuesday, green, deep and dark with bright outlines,
a pinewood at break of day.
A stream flowing, something I know,
dry leaves, a path that leads on.

The down side is an empty garage,
two old tyres, dampness in the air,
cans of oil and a birdcage.

Wednesday, mushroom coloured,
an eighteenth century *patisserie*
twinkling chandeliers and walls of pistachio.
I wish I had a novel to read.

Thursday, *Burnt Sienna*, I like Thursday,
it's dark and interesting.
I'm sitting by the fire dreaming of Coleridge.

Friday, burnt bacon and workmen's tea.
A gathering of strangers in the stranger's hall.
What's in my box? Cakes of paint
and vagabond shoes pointing to the door.

Saturday, orange and pink,
a lady should never despair about the colour of her nails,
her down-trodden heels or her rinsed hair.
The fridge is full.

Sunday, milky blue, like the *cote d'azur* on a winter's day.
Bells are ringing, for life or love –
leave the window open.

PARADELLE FOR KEATS

Keats, that room in Rome where you died
Keats, that room in Rome where you died
Was full of melancholy like an empty dairy
Was full of melancholy like an empty dairy
Rome was full. You melancholy, in an empty dairy
Like that room where Keats died.

The second floor of a strawberry pink house
The second floor of a strawberry pink house
Overlooking the square, the rusty palm trees
Overlooking the square, the rusty palm trees
A rusty pink, the second house, looking over
The square floor of the strawberry palm trees.

Whisper to me a secret feeling
Whisper to me a secret feeling
The blood from your lungs is breaking up
The blood from your lungs is breaking up
A secret is breaking, the lungs whisper up to me
Feeling from your blood.

You died in Rome, the second floor of
A pink house, over a square of melancholy.
Looking up, feeling an empty room,
The blood was like a strawberry breaking from your
Rusty lungs. The secret dairy, the palm trees
Whisper to me, where is that Keats?

COLERIDGE AT GRETA HALL, 1802

In your room everything breathes.
Slowly the coal burns,
as it shimmers its scarlet silks and slowly turns.

The hours solidify into amber,
a stag beetle sealed within,
with your filaments of flamey blue and green.

Your hive of midnight bees
is bursting with fatal stings,
Pegasus rears up and shakes them from his wings.

The moon hangs out the trees,
black lace over the stars,
but you just stare at the night like an animal behind bars.

We are separated by a chasm of time
which sucks out the heat of life
yet I still feel jealous of your love and pity for your wife.

SNOW AND PASTERNAK
reading *Dr. Zhivago* in the French Alps

Reading Pasternak,
his descriptions of snow and melting snow
and love and women and the dark interiors of old Russia,
I moved into the rooms after him,

or hurried through the terrible cold.
It was winter, and the sledge creaked and juddered
over the potholed road.
The smell of leather and horse sweat mixed

with the stiff old carriage fur. The hoof prints
glistered over the damask road
like roses leading to a palace of salt.
Streams rushed

in a ceaseless gush of white
and the fir trees were still and straight
under the weight of snow
as life flew past the horse's ears.

In the Spring the snow melted,
revealing the old yellow of winter.
The grass shoots began to unstick their limey threads
and bundles of green fizzed up through the pudding earth.

Before I knew it, Summer came with her heat and dust.
The road bent under the glare of copper light.
Wild roses beat a soft tattoo round
the apple trees in abandoned orchards.

Close by is the memory of war,
bottled up inside like poison gas,
of horrible hardship, sewing up body parts,
sterilising blades in an old billy-can.

The woodland still in leaf, the harvest coming in,
you are galloping over the fields, torn by the love of two women.
You hold reins, you hold the mane, you cry.
And the two women are everything any man ever needed...

FRANK SINATRA

Frank Sinatra,
the name itself is like a long romance.
The way you sang the words,
sweet as plums –
I wanted to climb inside your mouth.

You could have eaten me right up!
A singing father
with woebegone shoulders,
you made a cordial out of your 'O's.

If love is some kind of dissolving,
I wanted to melt into the vibrato of your vocal chords,
to be carried, to be carried in your arms.

But there was nobody there,
just the cold linen armchair,
the shiny cover of the long-playing record
and the curious pain of imagined love.

FRANK SINATRA DECONSTRUCTED

Fr-frill, a froth,
then *a* short and high, opening out,
a kind of happiness.
Then *nk* the *n* mute like a lackey
but the *k* sharp and explosive.
Sin one syllable, simple,
red to black.
The middle *a* is *legato*
the art of you
and the last *tra* is feminine and flouncy,
a question mark struck at the heart.

IF YOU NEVER GROW UP

If you never grow up, does it matter?
If the years stack up
In a tower of shells
That might fall
Scattering over the sand like lost buttons
Under which you crawl
Revealing how dark you are
How raw inside
Moving with such tiny steps across the moving tide.

If you never grow up, does it matter?
If the years ring out
Like old church bells
That still toll
Clanging above the square in iron hums
To where you stand
Unsure, glove in hand
And you are
Trapped, all your different selves, like minnows in a jar.

If you never grow up, does it matter?
If the years rack up
Like unknown hats
In a tailor shop
Calling out to strangers as they pass
And you look up
With your bedroom eyes
To discover that
You don't have to grow up to have a past.

FEAR OF FALLING

The sea is washing its sheets.
Through closed eyes
I hear the slap and suck
of it beating the fabric of itself,
its elastic wetness
pulsing against the rocks.
Glass that melts
over and over the rocky ledge,
hissing out a lacey frill,
a liquid edge.
Nothing on the surface
but sunlight and the slant of depths.
A rocking horse ocean
rocking the deep.
A sofa without a seat,
if I'm not careful,
I'll fall right through,
knocked out by emerald knuckledusters,
the weight of water,
electric blue.

LONDON BLUES

I have known the loneliness of furnished rooms
where the heart breaks in slow motion
like a Ming vase falling in a dream.

Smelling a stranger on my lover's skin
I turned myself out
I turned myself in

I wept under an eiderdown
in a room no bigger than a horse box
in Camden Town,
waiting for the knots to dissolve
along the tongue and groove of varnished pine.

In Finsbury Park I slept where I could,
glad to smother the hard corners of the hours
with the soft cloth of sleep.

In Chelsea and Cricklewood
I drew white lines with the London boys,
lounged about on beaten-up old sofas,
smoking joints and telling lies.
I sulked my way through days,
collar up, buttoned high,
I walked along the bridge of doubt.

In Crouch End
I have known the desolation of launderettes
where the service lady sat all afternoon folding
tobacco smoke into the hot, dried clothes,
her head bent before a small TV,
closing the porthole door with one hand
while smoke rose from the other
like strange blossom round a tree.

Next door the Asian newsagent with sad eyes
whose *Golden Virginia* must stand in
for the beauty of a sunrise.
I have known the last bus and the end of the line,
too much to drink and 'Gentlemen, Time.'

All this went on and on
till you came along in your old hat and coat
knocking on my door at the dead of night.
You broke down my tough little fence of independence,
held me in your arms by candlelight.
Then it was green, it was lilac, it was rain
and in Highgate Cemetery the stone angels
clapped their stone wings,
and raised me up to whisper things.

PARADISE BEACH

The bones of good and evil lie up to their waist in sand.

Every day the colour of the water changes,
sometimes it is bitter blue and green

revealing shards of flickering fish
and flattened fists of seaweed in its voluminous depths.

Other days it is cloudy, a broth of steel,
scumming a wavy line along the curved arm of beach.

A classic horse-shoe cove,
overlooked by scrub and rock and a white, bulbous church.

It holds its beauty modestly; like an ancient stoic
it has to bear the violations of 20th century life.

A north wind brings a flotilla of bottles, split cups,
silver crisp packets and other unbreakable things.

In the middle of the bay, there's a rock like a shark's fin,
arising from a swath of slippery ribbons with sea urchins

in a ring of soft black pins.
Twice I swim to it and climb on to its jagged ledges

like a clumsy mermaid triumphant at breaching
Neptune's imagined attack,

I talk to myself as I swim back.

One day, just before dusk,
I walk quickly down the road,
past three baby kittens mewling
from heart-shaped mouths.
Past fat Yani taking the weight off his dainty feet,
in his shop of red tins and brooms and vegetables
and salt fish and anything else you might need.
Past his donkey waiting by the wall
and the sharp yellow leaves of a dried thistle.
Past the hens roosting in the fig tree,
past the stiff legs of the hobbled cows with their troubled eyes.
Past all these distractions to the whispering sea:

Wait, wait for me!

I slip into the water
as the the sun drips rose petals
into the dust-coloured ocean
and the mountains are drawn
in electric lines of pink and gold.
On the beat of a bat's wing,
the beach lifts its lilac sails
and drifts towards the dark breath of night.

YANI'S PARLOUR

Outside the world was white hot.
Inner linings all burnt away.
Damp corners hoovered out by the sun's relentless in-breath.
A very few eye lashes of grass survived and the tousled
eucalyptus tree made a bustle of shade.

Yani's parlour was like a church, simple, holy and safe.
The table was spread with white lace, (protected by a
sheet of wipe-down, polka-dotted plastic) cloth flowers,
roses and wisteria, frothed over two cut glass vases.
Framed photos of a slick young man in an open shirt
and a woman wearing honky lipstick, her hair clumped
and shiny like a horse's mane. The children who had
left for Athens.

It's about 5.30 and the afternoon is turning slowly on
its heel. A last shot of liquid heat is thrown at the front
of the house. Two yellow silk curtains hanging over the
high windows translate the sunlight into shafts of maizey
gold. A length of sprigged white cotton floats across the
mouth of the door. The ceiling is painted blue.

And in that ship of shadows
we drifted and flew
from the sprigged sail filled with light
past the linen cupbards, empty beds,
to the heart of home,
where we looked out laughing
from the lap of a giant mother
and stroked the white cat
when it climbed up and looked at us with hard yellow eyes.

SONG TO HERMES

Cattle thief
Commander of dreams
Music maker
Unpicker of seams.

Slim as a boy
Guide to the dead
Faster than light
Better in bed.

A go-between
From the house on the hill
Where the Gods chill out
With time to kill.

Pretty as a girl
Quiet as a cat
A kind of informer
Joker in the pack.

Find me at the crossroads
Where old ghosts meet
Love of my life
On Hooky Street.

THE WEDDING

She put up her hands in alarm
And tried to hide in the cupboard.
They found her and marched her out.
Mother stood over her, but she didn't really care,
She looked out of the window,
Longing to be dead or in the garden
Anywhere but *here* dressing her daughter.
They made sense of it with paper flowers and stalks of corn.
There was a cake on stilts,
White as her own cow's milk in the pale.
The eyes of the grown ups
Swept her up and down.
Grandmother's silver on the table, now her own.
The trinkets she brought as part of her dowry,
Coins hot and cold in her lace pocket.
The bundle of linen,
Four sheets, four pillow-slips.
One rose brocade tablecloth heavy as water.
Wild strawberries in crystal cups still uneaten by dawn.
In the small, hot bedroom,
She fought for her life under the feather bed
But his hard, probing hands suddenly
Turned soft and stroked her back
With the tips of his wings.

FEBRUARY IS A GREEN MONTH

February is a green month,
a baby sweetness
about its bare shoulders.

All the beginnings of hope
in its clean, spare landscape:
a slight twist of hunger

in its empty fields,
the enclosed memory of stones.
Under the hedge,

a tremble of snowdrops.
Sunlight makes a plaid of gold,
wind and smoke.

Ivy shimmies round the hawthorn,
this is happiness,
the smell of earth.

SHE KEEPS THREE CATS

She keeps three cats, or they keep her,
like Russian women,
they seem to grow bigger at night.
A sumptious sheen on their glossy shoulders
and starlight in the aura of their fur.
Who needs a dog?
is merely implied by the silence.
The gracious haunch extends in a leg-of-mutton pose,
inner rhythms elide the need for formal exercise,
these junctions boxes of meditation
have all of their fuses earthed.

Installations of the most sophisticated sort,
they enhance their surroundings threefold.
One grows from the centre of the carefully made
spare bed, a magnificent hat sewn to the cover.
The other simmers orange hot like a small fox
on the deep brown top of the piano.
The last, like a forgotten stole, thrown down by the
telephone, sleeps intently.
While outside in the front garden birds fly
from bush to bush singing gently.

WATER AND STONES

There is common driftwood on every stream,
antlers, tree bones
torn from another life

though nothing is more beautiful than the patterns of water
silking round stones

the water that circles like a question mark
over my heart
is playing the same tune over and over

like the pluking of cold iron
desire is an old dog lying low under the yew tree
bound and unbound

while the stream trickles
clear, clear over Sussex clay
and when I was a child I understood

how water sang in rhythms
anonymously

over stones nestled into mud
breathing out grass roots and
yellow butterflies.

THE RAINY SEASON

It's raining hard
but nothing rains like the rain in Cambodia
falling on you like pins and needles
making you stiff with fright.

For days now we hear the constant
splashing against the window pane
the garden is drowning
under the whoosh of rain on rain.

And yet
nothing rains like the rain in Cambodia
where the weight of silver
annihilates your frame

and the ecstatic beats of water
make you want to pray
or hold your breath

watch bluebells bouncing on a tin roof

TUOL SLENG
Dedicated to Vann Nath

Of all the prisons, in all the world,
   this might be the worst
      since it lay in the heart of Phnom Penh city
         and consumed its people from the inside out.

It's the loneliness of being caught.
   The mortal sting
      of fear that opens up their eyes
         in such a vacant stare.

It's just a register, nothing more

The cruelty of the past
   haunts the building,
      collecting in invisible spores
         inside sawn-off petrol cans

once used for shit and piss,
   smeared like dust
      over the tiled floor
         or in the concrete corners of the empty school

rooms. Desolation in the dark brown
   doors hung open like
      broken jaws.
         The makeshift cells so quickly built

of breeze blocks and cement.   ·
   We walk past instruments of torture,
      nausea rising like a stream of consciousness
         Pol Pot, Pol Pot, Pol Pot.

In the searing heat of the courtyard
   a huge old tree gives shade.
      Barbed wire hangs in a stiff veil
         that once netted people alive.

The horses have bolted, the horses have gone

We are stung, but not fatally.
   We want to cry but we cannot.
      We are so sorry for ourselves,
         for the comfort we cannot bring.

CAMBODIAN SMILE

Don't ask me why
this dead end place should make me happy
in the early morning light

Battambang Airport
at the end of a dirt track,
the departure lounge

no bigger than a village hall,
lilac curtains blowing
like silk flags against the wall.

Perhaps I want to go back
to the 1950's
when men were men

and women wore lipstick
and tucked in their blouses.
Is it reading *The Quiet American*

that moves me to think
I am travelling somewhere special
where I have never been before?

Or is it that phenomenon, the Cambodian smile?
A cover up, a perfect foil,
a flower without form,

blooming so sweetly,
from the depths of the Vietnam War.

HOTEL ROYALE

White heat on the concrete, 90 degrees fahrenheit
dapples the deep aquamarine of the luxury pool,
blue lines draw the silk curtains shut against the light

inside the hotel room. Neither angel nor fool
could disregard the simple fact that we are man and wife
and over our own eyes we'll pull down the wool

that binds us like the strands of our shared life.
Our worries, our work, our wishes, protects as soft wire
strengthens the worn handle of an old kitchen knife;

and so against all the odds the secret pathways of fire
still find a way up through the mosaic surface of the day
to crack the stonework with tendrils of desire.

So kiss me, then, stroke my hair,
while we move, temporarily, beyond earthly despair.

NOW IN MY ENGLISH GARDEN

Now in my English garden
buttercups and clover hold up
bees and butterflies
swashbuckling the air currents
with tiny swords.
Scarlet geraniums
flake on to the brick path.
Even the roses, gone over,
cracked into brittle rags of brown
tell me everything I know about myself
and my home town.

Unlike the crimson pods of the flame trees
at the silkworm factory in *Siem Reap*
or the flagrant embroidery
of a bougainvillea
falling open like a kimono
in the heat.
The brown streets
flew up dust or puddled deep, deep,
holding memories
too deep to speak of,
without twisting the hot ribs of pain
into a mere morsel of fact.

Then something new entered
into my flat-packed heart
with a sing-song voice of a child.

LEAVING YOU

is like being torn away
from my tree, unpeeled
into the clattering night of strangers and blue lights.

There's a cavalcade of travellers
passing through a no-mans land of passport controls,
luggage checks and departure lounges.
Inside the airless cabin
the seat belt clasps me with a tinkle.

Down the corridor of arms,
there, in the green corner of your shoulder,
you can bury me under hot twigs
and the wallpaper will fade,
the curtains close their daylight eyes.

In a crowd of people we stand crying
for the hard core of love
that will not cool
but hurts us with boiling kisses
running down the ribs of time.

MEMOIRS OF AN OPIUM PIPE

I remember the first pair of hands that held me
and placed the fine spout to the lips:

a gentleman tailor from Phnom Penh,
his fingers soft as a girl's.

Smoke rose in a small coil
of oily yellow.

Small dragons nosed at my bowl,
cool feet in the dust.

The hours of the night broke
slowly like an old train going south.

Draw back the crimson sash,
let me drown in the gathering light.

MR. CUNG

We were two ladies in the noon day sun,
jolting over the pot-holed roads of Phnom Penh,
in a tok-tok (half motor bike, half van).

The sun shone on Mrs. Ada's bobbed white hair
and her swan-like neck,
it surprised me she never wore a hat.

We stopped on the corner of two small streets –
CUNG, TAILEUR, HOMME ET DAME –
with our bags of material swinging round our feet.

Mr. Cung was absurdly elegant, small and thin,
he wore baggy pants and a vest,
his face scratched with lines like an old tin.

Behind the red-felt curtain there were rolls of cloth,
dust, threads and a floor length mirror to stare in.
He took our measurements with the ghost of a smile,

his fingers fluttering over our figures
like butterflies over tall flowers.
What, if he knew you, he might have told:

They have taken everything from me,
my mother, my father,
even the small wooden house we lived in.

THE RAGS OF MY DREAMS

The rags of my dreams
Decorate the bare walls
With blisters of colour;
I will have cried that day,
I will have swept the floor then.
Sometimes things fall into place
With an unimagined sweetness,
My goodbye keys on the chair,
The copper waterfall of the beech tree falling outside
And the feelings inside
Growing like fibres in the woven cloth.
The postman slithers the letters through the letterbox,
They fall like a hand of cards upon the mat.
The cat licks herself patiently,
All wait for the dreams to come,
To be sewn with brilliant thread,
To lie around me like a cloak of love,
To keep me from the dead.

LAST SESSION

Lying on the Corbusier couch for the last time,
watching the clouds bump along
and you behind me in your chair,
your words still in the air:
an intimacy gained closer than
any lover or friend,
all the gaps that we've peered through
but never got to the end.
Goodbye is a lumpy, sparkling thing,
hanging above us in the sky.
The small room floats away
down a river of talk
and all that we don't say.

SISTERS

like having three mothers
fold back your hair

in the way we raise our eyes
and shut them for a long second.

We always smile at waiters.
We crave special relationships with doctors and nurses,
even the man behind the ticket office

blossoms under our eyes.
How we adore kindness!
Nothing less than kittenish,

we worship the postman
with his burden of paper mouths;
the last messenger on earth.

Lost and found by the fireside,
hormonally engaged
with our genetic hand-me-downs,

we are all soul
and no backbone and
our gravity is water, our roots are blood.

GHOSTS

Lightning wakes me, her lilac roots
striking me across the mouth of sleep

and something closes like a pleated skirt
when the legs have finished dancing.

Who blocked that little stammer
of ideas that were tiptoeing out?

(The white windows of day say nothing)

The heart lies in a strongbox,
not vulnerable to electric storms

but I know that love exists
in the humming of your arms about me,

in the footsteps of your fingertips
on my temple bones

sliding down the short strands of my hair
like field mice in the sun.

I sleep just below the surface,
just below the water, the ocean,
upside-down mirror of the day.
I dream of water, a roomful of people,
but I'm sitting in the wrong café.
There is no escape from death
whatever you do or say.
The years are made of paper,
you can bang them flat between your hands.

Now at the dead time when the world is up and running when the phones are ringing and the dish washer is thumping and school is half way through first period and people are waiting to see the dentist flicking through magazines a nervous shiver in the stomach hearing the faint high pitched whine of the high speed drill from the floor above when the receptionist clears her throat drinking her second cup of coffee and there is light music coming from somewhere and beyond the filmy net curtains the traffic has a serious sound to it and buses are revving and gliding over the streets of cities all over England when the washing is hung out to dry and the cows have all been milked long ago when mothers have left their toddlers at playgroup and the

tears and the tantrums are no longer thrumming the air
when the second batch of loaves is baked and cooling and
the first shift are off drinking tea and the long-distance lorry
drivers are pulling in to eat eggs and bacon and the full
caboosh now is the dead time when the cat sleeps and the
birds are silent and the sky is warmed up like silk pyjamas
by the pale winter sun now I –

All the footmen are disappearing,
the excitement of presents brought before me,
gifts at the table, vanish.
There's nothing left but the electric stick of the clock
tapping a pathway for me in the dark.
When the poems are shot dead
no one notices.
There's a rustle of shopping bags
or someone on Radio 4 is talking about tax relief.
The ghosts slide up and down the parapet,
mocking me with their dropped eyes,
their see-through bodies.
I hear their shrieks in the flattened voices of the television
or in the rushing air before a tube train.
Creatures forever on their way to execution,
they are my people.

*When I wake up shaken and stirred
I can't remember anything beautiful.*

*Dreams slip off my back like snakes
returning to the undergrowth.*

*Lightning wakes me, her lilac roots
striking me across the mouth of sleep;*

*it's not true what I said,
my heart is vulnerable to electric storms.*

In the afternoon,
the dead are buried deeper.
There are holes, soft bites into the bones
like coral in the sand
Maybe the sunlight hangs itself between the curtains,
stretching out to warm the hours.
For a while the flowers are thick with lustre and grace.
I might be consoled by a story or the intimate
jewelry of spoken words
but something turns over and falls away;
far inside me the twin towers of panic and boredom
rear their shear sides against the fragile day.

My own mother rings the doorbell
only by now I've lost my ticket to the dancehall
the entrance is one way
in the bowery
we eat rose petals
they have no taste
colour and sugar are one
when its all black
I wake up, gone

SWANS

The swans are gazing at themselves
tubular necks compressed
into a fat S.
The collapsed box of their wings
tipped together at the back
as if they hinged
upon the pond's black skin.
They gaze and swim and rest
the whole white question mark
ending in a soft-shoe beak of death.

Sometimes two blunder-buses take off:
necks like white snakes
they beat the air with ungainly wings,
heavy bundles of feather, bone and flesh,
they skid-mark the water
like water-skiers, breaking on black feet,
before letting their plump breasts down
into the black silk sheet.
Then they collect themselves in a shiver
of oily white and glide on.

VALENTINE

Knowing love as I really think I really
Do, I sometimes laugh like a baby seeing
Faces turn to and turning home to faces
    Lovely and yearning.

Love is always retuning home to its
sources, finding pathways and backward winding
Seams of water, divining rods and streams
    Uprising purely.

Turn me to you, then, surely, without loss of
Face, for heaven is only what we long for
Accidentally, face to face, childlike sometimes
    True as swan-song.